# USING
# MATHS

## DESIGN A ROLLER COASTER

by Hilary Koll, Steve Mills
and Korey T. Kiepert

ticktock

# USING
# MATHS
# DESIGN A ROLLER COASTER

Copyright © ticktock Entertainment Ltd 2006

First published in Great Britain in 2006 by ticktock Media Ltd.,

Unit 2, Orchard Business Centre, North Farm Road, Tunbridge Wells, Kent, TN2 3XF

ISBN 1 86007 985 7

Printed in China

A CIP catalogue record for this book is available from the British Library.

All rights reserved. No part of this publication may be reproduced, copied, stored in a retrieval system
or transmitted in any form or by any means electronic, mechanical, photocopying, recording or otherwise
without prior written permission of the copyright owner.

Hilary Koll (B.Ed. Hons) was a Leading Maths Teacher in a primary school before training as a Numeracy Consultant for the National Numeracy Strategy. She has worked as a Lecturer in Mathematics Education at the University of Reading, teaching on undergraduate, post-graduate and training courses. She is now a full-time writer and consultant in mathematics education. Hilary Koll and Steve Mills can be contacted via their website www.cmeprojects.com

Steve Mills (B.A. Hons, P.G.C.E., M.Ed.) was a teacher of both primary and secondary age children and an LEA Maths Advisory Support Teacher before joining the University of Reading as a Lecturer in Mathematics Education. He worked with both undergraduate and post-graduate students in their preparation for teaching maths in schools. He has written many mathematics books for both teachers and children. Visit www.cmeprojects.com for details.

Korey works at The Gravity Group, a firm that specialises in designing wooden roller coasters. He participates in the design and engineering of the roller coasters, and has worked on The Voyage at Holiday World & Splashin' Safari, Santa Claus, Indiana and Hades at Mt. Olympus Water & Theme Park, Wisconsin Dells, Wisconsin. Korey has a degree in Mechanical Engineering from the Michigan Technological University.

# CONTENTS

## NUMERACY WORK COVERED IN THIS BOOK:

**CALCULATIONS:**
Throughout this book there are opportunities to practise **addition, subtraction, multiplication** and **division** using both mental calculation strategies and pencil and paper methods.

**NUMBERS AND THE NUMBER SYSTEM:**
- COMPARING NUMBERS: pgs. 6, 7, 10, 11, 21, 27
- DECIMALS: pg. 11
- ESTIMATING: pgs. 22, 23, 27
- FRACTIONS: pgs. 12, 15
- ORDERING NUMBERS: pg. 7
- PLACE VALUE TO THE NUMBERS: pgs. 20, 21
- USING LARGE NUMBERS: pgs. 20, 21
- WRITING NUMBERS IN WORDS: pg. 20

**SOLVING 'REAL LIFE' PROBLEMS:**
- CHOOSING THE OPERATION: pgs. 10, 19
- MAPS: pgs. 9, 13
- TIME: pgs. 18, 19, 22, 23, 26

**HANDLING DATA:**
- GRAPHS: pgs. 26, 27
- USING TABLES: pgs. 7, 10, 11, 18, 19

**MEASURES:**
- AREA: pgs. 8, 12, 13
- PERIMETER: pgs. 8, 9, 16
- RELATIONSHIPS BETWEEN UNITS OF MEASUREMENT: pgs. 10, 11

**SHAPE AND SPACE:**
- 2-D SHAPES: pgs. 12, 13, 16, 24, 25
- ANGLES: pgs. 14, 15, 24
- GRID CO-ORDINATES: pg. 8
- SYMMETRY: pg. 24

**Supports the maths work taught at Key Stage 2 and 3**

# HOW TO USE THIS BOOK

**M**aths is important in the lives of people everywhere. We use maths when we play a game, ride a bike, go shopping – in fact, all the time! Everyone needs to use maths at work. You may not realise it, but a designer would use maths to plan and build a roller coaster! With this book you will get the chance to try lots of exciting maths activities using real life data and facts about roller coasters. Practise your maths skills and experience the thrill of what it's really like to design a coaster that will take your passengers on the most exciting ride of their lives.

**This exciting maths book is very easy to use – check out what's inside!**

Fun to read information about how a roller coaster is designed and built.

## KNOW YOUR COASTERS

**H**ow much do you know about roller coasters? Are you an expert? Do you know how high some of the tallest coasters are? Do you know which of the world's roller coasters give the longest ride? Which are fastest? Which roller coasters carry most people? Which are considered the most exciting? You will need to know all these things to be able to design your own roller coaster and make yours bigger and better than the rest. There are two different types of roller coasters: those made with steel tracks and those with wooden tracks. A **wooden coaster** has tracks made of wood, but the **structure** can be made with steel or wood.

## MATHS ACTIVITIES

Look for the **COASTER WORK.** You will find real life maths activities and questions to try.

To answer some of the questions, you will need to collect data from a DATA BOX. Sometimes, you will need to collect facts and data from the text or from charts and diagrams.

Be prepared! You will need a pen or pencil and a notebook for your workings and answers.

### COASTER WORK

In the DATA BOX you will see a table showing information about roller coasters around the world. Use the information in the table to help you answer these questions.

1) Which roller coaster in this list is:
   a) highest?
   b) fastest?
   c) longest?
   d) oldest?

2) How much taller is:
   a) Kingda Ka than The Beast?
   b) Top Thrill Dragster than Daidarasauras?
   c) Tower of Terror than The Voyage?

3) One coaster travels twice as fast as another coaster. Which two coasters are they?

4) How many years between the opening of:
   a) Dodonpa and The Voyage?
   b) The Ultimate and The Beast?
   c) The Big Dipper and Hades?

   *(You will find a TIP to help you with these questions on page 28)*

### COASTER HISTORY FACTS

The earliest roller coasters were Russian ice slides. People would sit in carved out blocks of ice and ride down wooden slides.

In the 1800s a railway was built in the USA to take coal downhill to a river. In the 1870s, when it was no longer used for coal, people enjoyed riding the **train** down the hillside.

The first real roller coaster opened in 1884 at Coney Island (New York, USA). It was called the Switchback Railway.

By 1930, there were 2000 roller coasters in the United States alone.

## DATA BOX

If you see one of these boxes, there will be important data inside that will help you with the maths activities.

MATHS ACTIVITIES

Feeling confident? Try these extra CHALLENGE QUESTIONS.

## IF YOU NEED HELP...

### TIPS FOR MATHS SUCCESS

On pages 28 – 29 you will find lots of tips to help you with your maths work.

### ANSWERS

Turn to pages 30 – 31 to check your answers.
(Try all the activities and questions before you take a look at the answers.)

### GLOSSARY

On page 32 there is a glossary of roller coaster words and a glossary of maths words. The glossary words appear in the text.

---

### DATA BOX — THE HIGHEST, FASTEST AND THE LONGEST COASTERS

Here is a list of some of the highest, fastest and longest roller coasters in the world.

Some are made from steel and are marked (S) and some have wooden rails and are marked (W)

| | Height (metres) | Top speed (miles per hour) | Length (metres) | Year open |
|---|---|---|---|---|
| The Beast, Ohio, USA (W) | 34 | 65 | 2256 | 1979 |
| Big Dipper, Blackpool, UK (W) | 18 | 42 | 1005 | 1923 |
| Daidarasauras, Japan (S) | 28 | 45 | 2340 | 1970 |
| Dodonpa, Japan (S) | 52 | 107 | 1189 | 2001 |
| Hades, Wisconsin, USA (W) | 42 | 65 | 1441 | 2005 |
| Kingda Ka, New Jersey, USA (S) | 139 | 12 | 8950 | 2005 |
| Millennium Force, Ohio, USA (S) | 91 | 92 | 2010 | 2000 |
| Top Thrill Dragster, Ohio, USA (S) | 128 | 120 | 853 | 2003 |
| Tower of Terror, Australia (S) | 115 | 100 | 376 | 1997 |
| The Ultimate, Lightwater Valley, UK (S) | 32 | 50 | 2270 | 1991 |
| The Voyage, Indiana, USA (W) | 49 | 67 | 1964 | 2006 |

---

### CHALLENGE QUESTION

Use the information in the DATA BOX above to help you answer these questions.

1) Put the list in order of the coasters' length, from shortest to longest.

2) How many coasters have a top
   a) greater than Hades?
   b) the same as Hades?
   c) less than Hades?

3) How many years after the Big Dipper was built were each of these rides built?
   a) The Beast
   b) Kingda Ka
   c) Millennium Force
   d) The Ultimate

Fascinating facts and tips about real-life roller coasters.

**H**ow much do you know about roller coasters? Are you an expert? Do you know how high some of the tallest coasters are? Do you know which of the world's roller coasters give the longest ride? Which are fastest? Which roller coasters carry most people? Which are considered the most exciting? You will need to know all these things to be able to design your own roller coaster and make yours bigger and better than the rest. There are two different types of roller coasters: those made with steel tracks and those with wooden tracks. A **wooden coaster** has tracks made of wood, but the **structure** can be made with steel or wood.

## COASTER WORK

In the DATA BOX you will see a table showing information about roller coasters around the world. Use the information in the table to help you answer these questions.

1) Which roller coaster in this list is:
   a) highest?
   b) fastest?
   c) longest?
   d) oldest?

2) How much taller is:
   a) Kingda Ka than The Beast?
   b) Top Thrill Dragster than Daidarasauras?
   c) Tower of Terror than The Voyage?

3) One coaster travels twice as fast as another coaster. Which two coasters are they?

4) How many years between the opening of:
   a) Dodonpa and The Voyage?
   b) The Ultimate and The Beast?
   c) The Big Dipper and Hades?

*(You will find a TIP to help you with these questions on page 28)*

### COASTER HISTORY FACTS

The earliest roller coasters were Russian ice slides. People would sit in carved out blocks of ice and ride down wooden slides.

In the 1800s a railway was built in the USA to take coal downhill to a river. In the 1870s, when it was no longer used for coal, people enjoyed riding the **train** down the hillside.

The first real roller coaster opened in 1884 at Coney Island (New York, USA). It was called the Switchback Railway.

By 1930, there were 2000 roller coasters in the United States alone.

Here is a list of some of the highest, fastest and longest roller coasters in the world.

Some are made from steel and are marked (S) and some have wooden rails and are marked (W)

| | Height (metres) | Top speed (miles per hour) | Length (metres) | Year open |
|---|---|---|---|---|
| The Beast, Ohio, USA (W) | 34 | 65 | 2256 | 1979 |
| Big Dipper, Blackpool, UK (W) | 18 | 42 | 1005 | 1923 |
| Daidarasauras, Japan (S) | 28 | 45 | 2340 | 1970 |
| Dodonpa, Japan (S) | 52 | 107 | 1189 | 2001 |
| Hades, Wisconsin, USA (W) | 42 | 65 | 1441 | 2005 |
| Kingda Ka, New Jersey, USA (S) | 139 | 128 | 950 | 2005 |
| Millennium Force, Ohio, USA (S) | 91 | 92 | 2010 | 2000 |
| Top Thrill Dragster, Ohio, USA (S) | 128 | 120 | 853 | 2003 |
| Tower of Terror, Australia (S) | 115 | 100 | 376 | 1997 |
| The Ultimate, Lightwater Valley, UK (S) | 32 | 50 | 2270 | 1991 |
| The Voyage, Indiana, USA (W) | 49 | 67 | 1964 | 2006 |

## CHALLENGE QUESTION
Use the information in the DATA BOX above to help you answer these questions.

1) Put the list in order of the coasters' length, from shortest to longest.

2) How many coasters have a top **speed**
   a) greater than Hades?
   b) the same as Hades?
   c) less than Hades?

3) How many years after the Big Dipper was built were each of these rides built?
   a) The Beast
   b) Kingda Ka
   c) Millennium Force
   d) The Ultimate

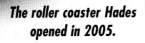

*The roller coaster Hades opened in 2005.*

**W**hen designing your roller coaster you must first decide on the size and shape of your plot of land. Some new roller coasters have to fit in between other rides at a theme park. You might have something in the middle of your plot of land that can't be moved, like a lake, a tree or a building. Once the plot has been chosen you can begin to design your coaster. Roller coasters are exciting because they make passengers feel they are speeding out of control. This is done using unexpected turns, drops and large 'hills' high above the ground. Going close to other rides in the park, or speeding past trees and large boulders on a mountainside also make rides exciting.

*Clearing the land*

## COASTER WORK

In the DATA BOX you will see maps of four different plots of land. Look closely at each map and answer these questions.

1) On which plot of land, A, B, C or D, is:
   a) a tree at the position (3, 1)?
   b) a lake at (2, 5)?
   c) a ride at (5, 3)?
   d) the entrance at (5, 6)?

2) What are the **coordinates** of:
   a) the tree in plot B?
   b) the lake in plot A?
   c) the entrance in plot D?
   d) the entrance in plot A?

*(You will find a TIP to help you with these questions on page 28)*

## CHALLENGE QUESTIONS

Look at the plots of land in the DATA BOX.

1) The **area** of plot A is 28 squares. What are the areas of the other three plots of land?
2) Which of the plots do you think has the longest perimeter?
3) Put the plots in order of size according to their approximate perimeters, with the shortest perimeter first.

*(You will find a TIP to help you with this question on page 28)*

## PLOT FACTS

Sometimes there are planning requirements and other factors that designers need to be aware of:
• Is there a rule saying how far you have to be from the edge of the plot?
• Is there a height restriction?
• Is the ground solid enough to be able to support the **structure** or is it soft ground?

## DATA BOX ) DIFFERENT PLOTS OF LAND

Here are some pictures of different plots of land that you could build your coaster on. There are advantages and disadvantages to them all.

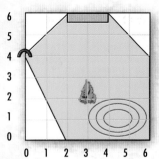

### Plot A
The first plot has a large mound which could be used as part of the ride. This would make the coaster cheaper to build because you would not need to construct as tall a hill to still get a big drop.

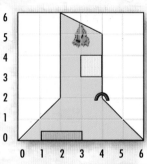

### Plot B
This plot is smaller and doesn't have a natural mound, so all hills would need to be made, costing more. It is the smallest plot and has many obstacles for the ride to avoid. There is another large ride which is part of the plot together with buildings, a lake and a tree.

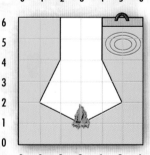

### Plot C
A plot like this one would be ideal for an '**out and back**' ride. This is a ride where you travel along, turn around and then go back. There are usually fewer twists and turns but lots of different sized hills. The rider would enjoy plenty of **airtime** (weightlessness).

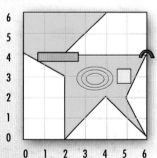

### Plot D
The fourth plot is an unusual shape and has several restrictions. The mound in Plot D is in the centre of the plot and might make it difficult to use as part of the coaster. The position of the buildings means that the ride would need to go over the top of them.

### Key

| Tree | Other Rides | Entrance |
|---|---|---|
| Mound | Buildings | Lake |

# HOW ROLLER COASTERS WORK

The ride on a coaster is not powered by an engine. The coaster is pulled to the top of a high hill and then the whole ride works because of **gravity**. The first hill, called the **lift hill**, must be the highest of them all. When a coaster speeds down one hill it will have the energy to make it up and over the next hill, if that hill isn't as high as the previous one. A roller coaster gradually slows down because of something called **friction**. Friction happens inside the wheels and where the wheels touch the track and cause the coaster to slow down a little. Roller coaster rides are exciting because of the **speed** and the twists and turns. Learn more about this here.

*The lift hill*

## COASTER WORK

It is vital that a roller coaster's first hill – called the lift hill – is the highest. Look at the designs in the DATA BOX.

Which of these designs do you think will work? Check to see whether the lift hill in each design is the highest. Remember to convert from centimetres to metres when you are comparing the heights.

*(You will find a TIP to help you with this question on page 28)*

## COASTER SCIENCE

When you are in a car that is going fast around a bend, did you ever notice how your body wants to lean towards the outside of the curve? That is because of forces that are placed on your body because you are travelling in what is called 'circular motion'. The force that is pushing you towards the outside of the circle is called '**centrifugal force**'. The faster you go around the turn, the stronger this force will be. Centrifugal force makes roller coasters more fun.

Here are five roller coaster designs, showing the height of each of their hills.

| Design | Lift hill | 2nd hill | 3rd hill | 4th hill |
|--------|-----------|----------|----------|----------|
| 1 | 87 m | 4200 cm | 9000 cm | 32 m |
| 2 | 10,000 cm | 76 m | 50 m | 2000 cm |
| 3 | 5020 cm | 52 m | 540 cm | 12 m |
| 4 | 6500 cm | 60.5 m | 6000 cm | 3500 m |
| 5 | 72.8 m | 5000 cm | 4360 cm | 50 m |

## CHALLENGE QUESTIONS

Look at design 5 in the DATA BOX.

1) How much higher is the first hill than the:
   a) second hill?
   b) third hill?
   c) fourth hill?
Give your answers in centimetres, and then in metres.

2) Convert 72.8 m into each of the following units:
   km        cm         mm

*(You will find a TIP to help you with these questions on page 28)*

## COASTER FACTS

Many roller coasters pull **cars** up a large hill to start the ride. Some use motors (attached to the track) that shoot a car out of the base station at high speed. Others use **hydraulic** or air cylinders to launch a car from the station at high **speed**.

**N**ow that you know how they work, it's time to start thinking about your design. When a coaster is being planned, a designer will make many drawings and think about whether the ideas would work to make an exciting ride. Here are some different designs to think about. Which do you think would make the most exciting ride? Your coaster needs to fit in with existing rides at the theme park. You need to decide whether your roller coaster will be low to the ground with lots of fast **'bunny hops'** (short fun hills), or whether you want a ride with more big **'airtime'** hills but a slower average **speed**.

## COASTER WORK

### Look at the plots in the DATA BOX.

The shape of Plot A shown in the DATA BOX is a hexagon as it has 6 sides. What is the name of the shape of Plot D?

What are the names of each of these shapes?

Count how many sides each has to help you decide.

## CHALLENGE QUESTIONS

Plot C covers 24 out of the 36 squares of the grid. We can show this as the fraction $^{24}/_{36}$.

1) Write 5 other fractions that are **equivalent** to $^{24}/_{36}$.

2) What is $^{24}/_{36}$ in its simplest form?

3) What is the fraction of the grid covered by Plot A? Write the fraction in its simplest form.

4) Write 5 other **fractions** that are equivalent to this.

*(You will find a TIP to help you with these questions on page 28)*

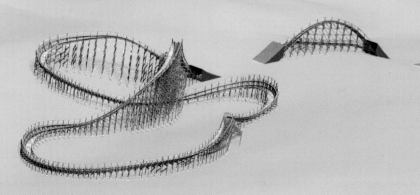

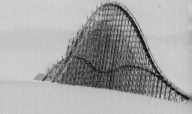

*A computer generated model showing the hills and tunnels on the coaster Voyage.*

## DATA BOX · DESIGNS OF ROLLER COASTERS

Here are some designs of roller coasters drawn from above.
Each ride is about the same length and has the same maximum height.

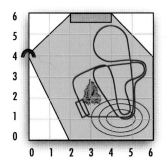

### Ride A

This ride features many **cross-overs**. Cross-overs make riders feel like they are going to hit the ride **structure** before ducking over or under it. After the first valley, there is a high hill called a **camelback**, called this because it looks like the hump of a camel. It gives a feeling of weightlessness. The final part of the ride includes a series of right and left turns with bunny hops in the straight sections of track.

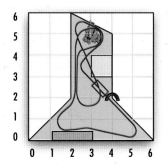

### Ride B

At the top of the **lift hill** there is a sharp turn before a straight drop. Later there is then a 'fan curve' to the left. You start low and then the track rises until the middle of the curve, where you start dropping again. After a spiral climb there is a drop off a hill, particularly good for those at the back of the **train**. A series of small bunny hops takes the coaster towards the lake, making a sharp left turn just before it.

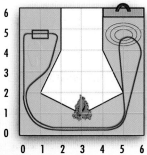

### Ride C

This ride is a **dog-legged** out-and-back coaster. On the way out it has big drops with long periods of airtime. There are many smaller bunny hop hills on the way home. Because they are smaller they would be faster, helping the rider not to feel that the ride is slowing down. There are fewer turns on this kind of ride. Instead, the ups and downs give it lots of 'airtime' (the feeling of weightlessness).

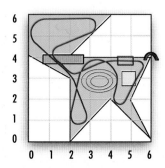

### Ride D

After leaving the station you make a sharp turn before climbing the lift hill. There is a horseshoe turn at the top of the lift, but the big drop is after the turn. After a long straight section of track there is a big camelback hill.

A series of bunny hops takes the roller coaster over the top of the building. A low, fast zig-zag section with bunny hops leads into the brake run.

---

**Key**

| | | | |
|---|---|---|---|
| Tree | Other Rides | Entrance | Station where people get on and off |
| Hill | Buildings | Lake | Roller coaster route — |

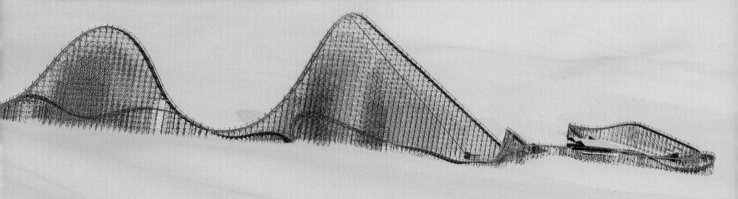

**W**hen you plan your roller coaster you need to add different twists, turns, drops and climbs to your ride. It is important that the ride doesn't do any one thing for too long a time. There are lots of terms to describe the twists and turns of a roller coaster, such as the corkscrew (a **loop** with a twist) or the Pretzel (a complicated twist that has shape of a pretzel). The corkscrew can now be found on many rides, but it wasn't until 1975 that the first corkscrew coaster was opened in California. Think carefully about how to combine all of the different elements of a ride. All these features in a ride add to the out-of-control feeling when you're on it!

## COASTER WORK
Look at the corkscrews in the DATA BOX.

1) Through how many **degrees** would you turn on:
   a) corkscrew A?
   b) corkscrew B?
   c) corkscrew C?

2) Through how many right angles would you turn on:
   a) corkscrew A?
   b) corkscrew B?
   c) corkscrew C?

*(You will find a TIP to help you with these questions on page 29)*

## COASTER FACTS

'**Airtime**' is the term used to describe that "butterflies in your stomach" weightless feeling that you have as you come over a hill on a roller coaster. A new coaster, The Voyage, is being designed to have the most airtime of any **wooden coaster** on the planet – over 24 seconds of airtime.

## DATA BOX  CORKSCREWS

Some coasters have loops one after another. These are sometimes known as corkscrews.

Here is some information about how many complete turns several different corkscrews have:

Corkscrew A     4 complete **revolutions**
Corkscrew B     6 complete revolutions
Corkscrew C     5 complete revolutions

A complete revolution is 360°. There are 4 **right angles** in one complete turn.

## OUT-AND-BACK DESIGNS

Many roller coasters use the **out-and-back** layout. These coasters have less twists and turns, but the hills give lots of ups and downs and feelings of weightlessness.

start

### Traditional
This ride takes you straight out and straight back. The tracks are close together so they can use the same **structure**. There are big hills on the way out and smaller, fast hops on the way home.

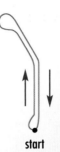
start

### Double
Used to fit an out-and-back ride onto a smaller plot. You go out, back, and then out and back again. The shared structure makes it cheaper to build.

### Dog-leg
An out-and-back ride with a bend in the middle. This is used to avoid buildings, trees and other rides.

start

## CHALLENGE QUESTION
### Can you complete this table?

| Twist turns you through | What **fraction** of a full turn is this? | What is the fraction in its smallest form? |
|---|---|---|
| 90° | $\frac{90}{360}$ | ¼ |
| 270° | | |
| 45° | | |
| 60° | | |
| 30° | | |
| 15° | | |

*A corkscrew turn*

**R**oller coasters made of steel are better for making complicated **loops** and turns, often turning the riders upside down. All loops are formed from the same basic shape, which looks like an upside-down teardrop. This shape is the most comfortable for the riders and allows the roller coaster to go faster. Another element you might want to add to your roller coaster design is a tunnel. The darkness of tunnels and the noise inside add to the feeling of **speed**. Changes in direction and sudden drops are scarier in tunnels because you can't see where you are or what will happen next.

## COASTER WORK

### Here are pictures of some loops.

To **estimate** how much track is needed for a loop we can draw two **polygons**. One is drawn inside the loop and one outside, as shown below. If you find the perimeter of each polygon you'll know that the length of the track will be between your two answers.

1) Find out the perimeter of the polygons in Loop A.

Inside      Outside

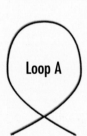

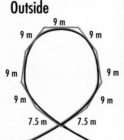

2) Find out the perimeter of the polygons in Loop B.

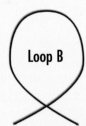

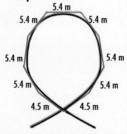

*(You will find a TIP to help you with these questions on page 29)*

## TUNNEL FACTS

On the Hades ride (Wisconsin Dells, USA), you dive into a tunnel straight after the **lift hill**. From the top of the lift hill, riders look down at a tiny black hole which gets larger and larger as they speed towards it. This tunnel takes them under a car park in total darkness with many small hops and turns.

## LOOP HISTORY

The Flip Flap Railway, built in 1901, was the first coaster with a loop. The ride was quickly closed because it was so uncomfortable!

When it was opened in 2000, Son of Beast was the only **wooden roller coaster** with a loop.

*Constructing the track in a tunnel. The **train** will tilt 90° in complete darkness.*

## CHALLENGE QUESTION

Use the two pairs of answers you found to the COASTER WORK questions.

If the length of each loop was exactly halfway between your two answers, how long would each loop be?

*(You will find a TIP to help you with this question on page 29)*

**Y**ou'll need to think about how many people you'd like your roller coaster to carry and to decide how long the ride will be. If you want to make money from your coaster then you need to get as many people as possible to come on your ride. If you ran a coaster that only took 10 people and lasted 20 minutes then you wouldn't make much money! Most roller coaster rides last 2-3 minutes with 20-30 people per **train**. There can also be more than one train: while one train is running the other can be letting passengers get on and off. The maximum number of passengers will depend on the type of train you buy from the manufacturers.

## COASTER WORK

In the DATA BOX you will see a table showing information about three different rides.

1) Which ride carries the most people in each train?

2) Which ride takes the longest time?

3) How many rides can there be per hour (60 minutes) for:
   a) Ride A?
   b) Ride B?
   c) Ride C?
   d) Ride D?

*(You will find a TIP to help you with these questions on page 29)*

### MULTIPLE TRAIN COASTER FACTS

To increase the number of people that can ride on a roller coaster, multiple trains can be used. A computerised control system is used to keep rides with multiple trains operating safely. A ride is split into zones. Trains have to be separated from each other by at least one zone. The control system will prevent a train from entering a zone until it is clear.

## DATA BOX    THE TRAIN

A roller coaster **train** is usually made from several **cars**.
Each car has several benches to sit on.
The benches usually seat 2 or 3 people.
This picture shows a train with 2 people per bench,
2 benches per car and 4 cars per train.

A park operator wants to put in a new ride, but he wants as
many people as possible to be able to go on the ride each
hour. The designer offers him four rides to choose from.

|        | People per bench | Benches per car | Cars per train | Ride time |
|--------|------------------|-----------------|----------------|-----------|
| Ride A | 2                | 2               | 6              | 3 minutes |
| Ride B | 2                | 3               | 5              | 4 minutes |
| Ride C | 3                | 2               | 3              | 2 minutes |
| Ride D | 2                | 4               | 4              | 5 minutes |

## CHALLENGE QUESTIONS

Use the information in the DATA BOX to find the maximum
number of people per hour that can travel on each of the rides.

1) The park operator wants as many people as possible to be able to go on the
ride each hour. Which ride should he choose?
2) Which ride takes fewest people per hour?

*(You will find a TIP to help you with these questions on page 29)*

**N**ow you've decided on your design, you must start thinking about ordering the materials. You will need to order thousands of steel bars and bolts to construct the ride. The bars are bolted together like a toy construction set. Now is the time to hire the site overseer, who will control the construction of the roller coaster. Your site overseer will need to hire all the machines needed to build the coaster: diggers, cranes, concrete mixers and so on. The coaster **structure** is put together on the ground and then a crane winches it into place. Your roller coaster is beginning to take shape!

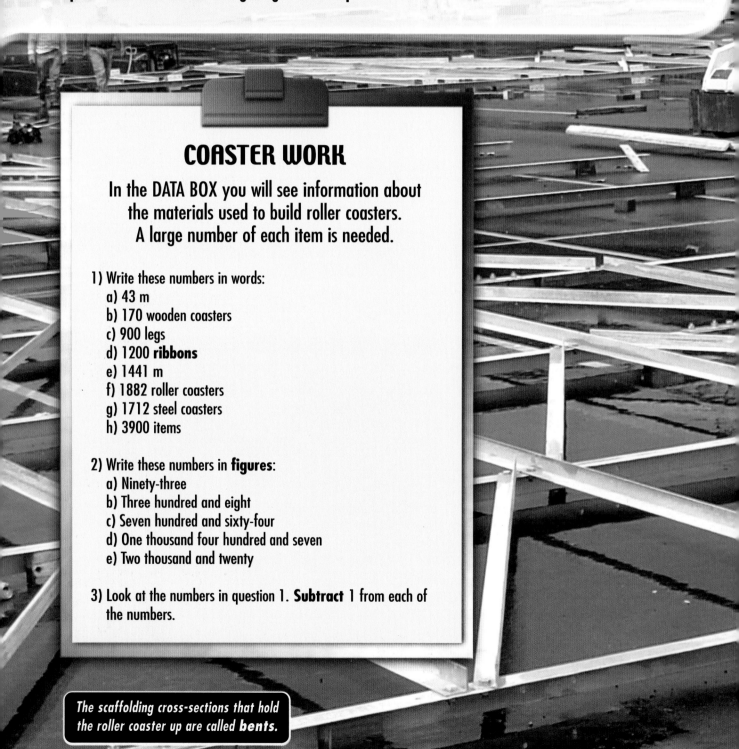

## COASTER WORK

In the DATA BOX you will see information about the materials used to build roller coasters.
A large number of each item is needed.

1) Write these numbers in words:
   a) 43 m
   b) 170 wooden coasters
   c) 900 legs
   d) 1200 **ribbons**
   e) 1441 m
   f) 1882 roller coasters
   g) 1712 steel coasters
   h) 3900 items

2) Write these numbers in **figures**:
   a) Ninety-three
   b) Three hundred and eight
   c) Seven hundred and sixty-four
   d) One thousand four hundred and seven
   e) Two thousand and twenty

3) Look at the numbers in question 1. **Subtract** 1 from each of the numbers.

*The scaffolding cross-sections that hold the roller coaster up are called **bents**.*

# BUILDING MATERIALS

On average, for every 3 m along a ride there is a cross-section that holds the track in place. Each cross section has 3 legs, 3 chords, 3 diagonals and 4 ribbons (thin bars). For a 900 m long ride you would need to order 900 legs, 900 chords, 900 diagonals and 1200 ribbons, making a total of 3900 items. This doesn't include the bolts, several other small metal pieces, or the track itself!

Hades is a 1441 m long roller coaster with a drop of 43 m. To build this ride, about 27,000 pieces of steel were used, weighing over 440,000 kg. 57,000 bolts were used to join the structure together.

Today there are approximately 1882 roller coasters operating worldwide. 1712 of these rides are steel coasters, with only 170 **wooden roller coasters**.

## COASTER FACTS

There are three wheels that run on the track of a roller coaster. The road wheel runs on the top of the track; the side wheel runs along the track; and the upstop wheel runs along the underside of the track. Together these three wheels ensure that the coaster **cars** will travel safely along the track.

## CHALLENGE QUESTIONS

1) For each of these numbers, give the value of the **bold** digit, e.g. in **4**3 the 4 stands for forty, and in **2**300 the 2 stands for two thousand.

   Use these column headings to help you:

| HTh | TTh | Th | H | T | U | |
|-----|-----|----|----|----|----|----|
|  | 2 | 7 | 0 | 0 | 0 | pieces of steel |
|  | 5 | 7 | 0 | 0 | 0 | bolts |
| 4 | 4 | 0 | 0 | 0 | 0 | kg |

   a) 1**4**41 m
   b) **1**882 roller coasters
   c) 1**7**12 steel coasters
   d) **3**900 items
   e) 2**7**,000 pieces of steel
   f) **5**7,000 bolts
   g) **4**40,000 kg

2) Look at the numbers in question 1. Divide each of the numbers by 10.

**N**ow the materials have arrived you must start the difficult work of building the roller coaster. You will need lots of workers to build the hills and tunnels. You will also need some skilled people to lay the tracks and cross-sections. A medium-sized **wooden roller coaster** takes about nine months to build. You will need to plan the timing of the construction work carefully. Most amusement parks are only open during the summer so you have the winter months to build the ride. This means building during the cold, wet months. Most theme parks want to open a new roller coaster to the public at the start of the summer season.

## COASTER WORK

In the DATA BOX you will see information about how long each part of the building work might take. Use this to help you **ESTIMATE** the length of time it would take for all jobs to be completed one after another. Give your answer in weeks.

Be careful — some times are given in weeks and some are given in months. Think of a month as about 4 weeks.

## CHALLENGE QUESTIONS

Look at your answer to the COASTER WORK on page 22.

1) How many days would it take for all of the jobs to be completed one after another?

2) Is your answer closest to:
   1 year?
   1½ years?
   2 years?

*(You will find a TIP to help you with these questions on page 29)*

### COASTER FACT

Sometimes as a coaster is being built parts of it might be changed. On the Hades ride, both the approach to the **lift hill** and the ending of the ride were changed after the turnaround (the halfway point, where the ride starts to go back to the finish) had been built.

## DATA BOX

## STAGES OF THE BUILDING WORK

Below are some times for each stage of the building work. Some of these jobs may be done at the same time.

**1) Survey**

1–2 weeks of surveying the site and laying out where the ride will go.

**2) Foundations**

3 months of people digging the foundations.

**3) Structure**

6 months including making the pieces of the coaster, taking them to the site, building the **structure** and tightening bolts.

**4) Tracking**

2–3 months of a crew of people stacking layers of wood, cutting the track and adding the track steel.

**5) Mechanical**

4 weeks installing brakes, queue gates, chain, motor and control system.

**N**ow that your roller coaster is built it is very important that it is tested for safety. You must carry out numerous tests to be sure that it will pass the safety review carried out by the inspectors. You may also want to conduct a trial run to make sure that the ride is an exciting one! Is there anything else you can do to make the coaster thrilling for the riders? Now is also the time to decide how much to charge for a ride. If you make the cost too high people might not go on the ride, but if you make it too cheap you might not make much money. Some theme parks simply charge an overall entrance fee, and each ride is free to use.

## COASTER WORK

In the DATA BOX you will see pictures of the structure of a roller coaster. You can see lots of different shapes made by the track support.

Here is a sketch of part of the support. Different shapes are marked in different colours in the picture.

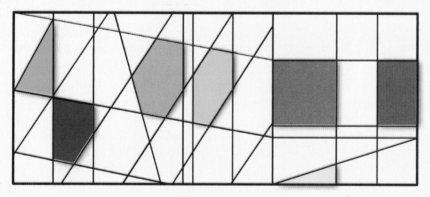

1) Can you name each of the shapes?
2) Which of the shapes have at least one **right angle**?
3) Which of the shapes have at least one line of symmetry?

*A coaster runs around another ride in a theme park.*

**BUILD FOR STRENGTH**

These pictures show a roller coaster under construction. The **structure** forms triangles for maximum strength.

## CHALLENGE QUESTION

Look at this picture.

How many triangles of different sizes can you see?

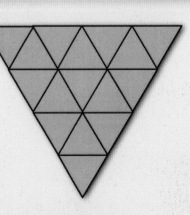

*(You will find a TIP to help you with these questions on page 29)*

**B**efore the roller coaster opens, safety inspectors examine the ride. They look at how people will get on and off the coaster and the safety precautions that are taken while the ride is running. The inspectors will check the **restraints** particularly carefully. The restraints secure passengers inside the **cars** during the ride. They might be lap bars or shoulder harnesses. The inspectors may put a height or age restriction on the ride so that very small children will not be in danger. For many rides in the USA you need to be at least 122 cm tall. The inspectors approve your design. You can now open your coaster to the public. Congratulations!

## COASTER WORK

In the DATA BOX you will see a graph showing a person's height above the ground as they go along the ride.

Use the graph to help you answer these questions:
1) How high above the ground is the person after
   a) 1 second?
   b) 4 seconds?
   c) 9½ seconds?
   d) 5 seconds?

2) About how many seconds after the start of the ride was the person at
   a) 50 metres?
   b) 3 metres?

3) The rider was 40 m above the ground three times during the ride. How many times was the person at a height above ground of
   a) 45 metres?
   b) 35 metres?
   c) 30 metres?
   d) 10 metres?
   e) 4 metres?

*Your roller coaster will provide a thrilling experience for millions of people.*

# THE INSPECTOR'S REPORT

Inspectors come to look at your coaster. They make lots of notes and measurements and make this graph to show a person's height above the ground as they go along the ride.

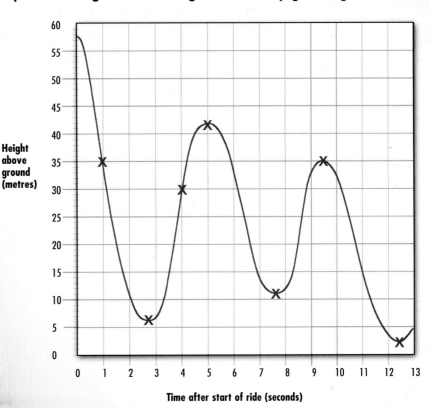

Height above ground (metres)

Time after start of ride (seconds)

## COASTER FACT

You can tell whether people have enjoyed the ride by listening to what they say as they get off. People who build coasters say 'The success of a ride can be measured in smiles'.

## CHALLENGE QUESTIONS

Use the graph in the DATA BOX to help you answer these questions:

The graph shows part of a ride with three hills.
1) About how high is each of the hills?
2) How much lower is the second hill than the first hill?
3) How much lower is the third hill from the second hill?
4) **Estimate** the height of the coaster after :
   a) 3.9 seconds
   b) 6.9 seconds
   c) 4.2 seconds
   d) 10.5 seconds

# TIPS FOR MATHS SUCCESS

## PAGES 6–7

Subtract the older date from the more recent date. For example, 2003–1997 = 6

## PAGES 8–9

### Using coordinates:

To find the coordinates of a point on a grid, you read the numbers along the bottom of the grid first and then the numbers upward along the side of the grid. The phrase 'Along the corridor and up the stairs' can help you to remember this.

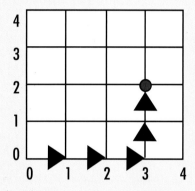

For example, (3, 2) means 3 steps along the bottom and then 2 steps up.

### CHALLENGE QUESTION

The perimeter of a shape is the distance all the way around the edge of it.

To find the area of an irregular shape count the number of whole squares inside the outline and then count the part squares. Buildings and other features that are inside the plot count as part of the area.

This shape has an area of 6 cm².

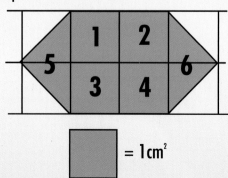

= 1cm²

## PAGES 10–11

### Changing metres to centimetres:

Remember that there are 100 centimetres in one metre, so to change from centimetres to metres divide by 100. To divide a number by 100 move each of the digits of the number 2 places to the right. For example: 57,960 ÷ 100 = 579.6

| Tth | Th | H | T | U | . t |
|-----|----|----|----|----|-----|
| 5 | 7 | 9 | 6 | 0 | |
| | 5 | 7 | 9 | 6 | |
| | | 5 | 7 | 9 | . 6 |

### Changing centimetres to metres:

Remember that there are 100 centimetres in one metre, so to change from metres to centimetres multiply by 100. To multiply a number by 100 move each of the digits of the number 2 places to the left. We use zeros to fill any empty columns. For example: 637.4 x 100 = 63,740

| Tth | Th | H | T | U | . t |
|-----|----|----|----|----|-----|
| | | 6 | 3 | 7 | . 4 |
| | 6 | 3 | 7 | 4 | |
| 6 | 3 | 7 | 4 | 0 | |

## PAGES 12–13

### CHALLENGE QUESTION

Some fractions look different but actually stand for the same amount. All these fractions have the same amount of the rectangle shaded. We say they are equivalent.

²⁄₄

³⁄₆

⁴⁄₈

⁵⁄₁₀

To make an equivalent fraction (one that is worth the same amount) you can multiply or divide the top and bottom numbers by the same number, like this:

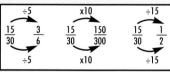

All these numbers are equivalent and ½ is the fraction in its simplest form as it cannot be made with smaller whole numbers on the top or bottom.

## PAGES 14–15

### COASTER WORK

Making turns and measuring angles:
An angle is a measure of turn. Angles are measured in degrees. The symbol for degrees is °. One whole turn (a complete revolution) is 360°. A quarter turn is 90°, or one right angle. There are four right angles in one whole turn.

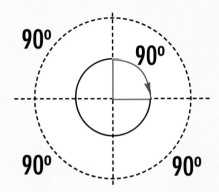

## PAGES 16–17

### COASTER WORK

The perimeter of a shape is the distance all the way around its edge.

### CHALLENGE QUESTION

To find a number that lies halfway between two others, first add them together and then halve the answer.
For example to find the number that lies halfway between 25 and 63, add 25 and 63.
25 + 63 = 88
Now halve the answer.
88 ÷ 2 = 44.
So 44 is exactly halfway between 25 and 63.

## PAGES 18–19

### COASTER WORK

To find how many people will fit on each train ride, multiply the number of people on each bench by the number of benches in each car, and then multiply by the number of cars in each train.
To find out how many rides can take place in one hour, remember that there are 60 minutes in one hour. Divide 60 minutes by how long each ride takes.

### CHALLENGE QUESTION

To find how many people can go on each ride in each hour, multiply the number of people on each train (answers to question 1) by the number of rides per hour (answers to question 3).

## PAGES 22–23

### CHALLENGE QUESTION

To change weeks into days multiply the number of weeks by 7.
10 weeks = 70 days,  20 weeks = 140 days and so on.
Remember that there are 365 days in a year (366 in a leap year).

## PAGES 24–25

### CHALLENGE QUESTION

Try to be systematic when looking for the triangles. Start by counting the very small triangles. Then look for slightly larger triangles and so on. A system will help make sure you don't miss any triangles out.

## PAGES 6–7

### COASTER WORK

| 1) | 2) | 3) | 4) |
|---|---|---|---|
| a) Kingda Ka | a) 105 m | The Ultimate, | a) 5 years |
| b) Kingda Ka | b) 100 m | Tower of Terror | b) 12 years |
| c) Daidarasauras | c) 66 m | | c) 82 years |
| d) Big Dipper | | | |

### CHALLENGE QUESTION

**1)**
Tower of Terror
Top Thrill Dragster
Kingda Ka
Big Dipper
Dodonpa
Hades
The Voyage
Millennium Force
The Beast
The Ultimate
Daidarasauras

**2)**
a) 6 coasters
b) 1 coaster
c) 3 coasters

**3)**
a) The Beast 56 years
b) Kingda Ka 82 years
c) Millennium Force 77 years
d) The Ultimate 68 years

## PAGES 8–9

### COASTER WORK

1) a) Plot C   b) Plot D   c) Plot D   d) Plot C
2) a) (3, 5)   b) (1, 4)   c) (6, 4)   d) (0, 4)

### CHALLENGE QUESTION

1) Area of plot   A = 28 squares   B = 15 squares
                  C = 24 squares   D = 17 squares
2) Plot C
3) Plot A, Plot B, Plot D, Plot C

## PAGES 10–11

### COASTER WORK

Designs 2 and 5 will work. In each of the other designs one of the other hills is larger than the first (lift) hill. This shows the table with all the measurements written in metres.

| Design | Lift hill | 2nd hill | 3rd hill | 4th hill |
|---|---|---|---|---|
| 1 | 87 m | 42 m | 90 m | 32 m |
| 2 | 100 m | 76 m | 50 m | 20 m |
| 3 | 50.2 m | 52 m | 5.4 m | 12 m |
| 4 | 65 m | 60.5 m | 60 m | 3500 m |
| 5 | 72.8 m | 50 m | 43.6 m | 50 m |

### CHALLENGE QUESTION

| 1) a) 2280 cm | 22.8 m | 2) 0.0728 km |
|---|---|---|
| b) 2920 cm | 29.2 m | 7280 cm |
| c) 2280 cm | 22.8 m | 72 800 mm |

## PAGES 12–13

### COASTER WORK

1) Plot D is a decagon.

| Triangle | | Quadrilateral | |
|---|---|---|---|
| Pentagon | | Hexagon | |
| Heptagon | | Octagon | |
| Nonagon | | Decagon | |

### CHALLENGE QUESTIONS

1) Any fractions that are equivalent to $\frac{24}{36}$ such as $\frac{2}{3}$, $\frac{6}{9}$, $\frac{12}{18}$, $\frac{10}{15}$, $\frac{48}{72}$, $\frac{240}{360}$, $\frac{2400}{3600}$ etc.

2) $\frac{2}{3}$

3) $\frac{1}{9}$

4) Any fractions that are equivalent to $\frac{7}{9}$ such as $\frac{14}{18}$, $\frac{21}{27}$, $\frac{28}{36}$, $\frac{35}{45}$, $\frac{70}{90}$, $\frac{700}{900}$ etc.

## PAGES 14–15

### COASTER WORK

**1)**
a) 1440°
b) 2160°
c) 1800°

**2)**
a) 16
b) 24
c) 20

### CHALLENGE QUESTION

| Twist turns you through | What fraction of a full turn is this? | What is the fraction in its smallest form? |
|---|---|---|
| 90° | $\frac{90}{360}$ | $\frac{1}{4}$ |
| 270° | $\frac{270}{360}$ | $\frac{3}{4}$ |
| 45° | $\frac{45}{360}$ | $\frac{1}{8}$ |
| 60° | $\frac{60}{360}$ | $\frac{1}{6}$ |
| 30° | $\frac{30}{360}$ | $\frac{1}{12}$ |
| 15° | $\frac{15}{360}$ | $\frac{1}{24}$ |

## PAGES 16–17

### COASTER WORK

1) 52 m and 78 m
2) 31.2 m and 46.8 m

### CHALLENGE QUESTION

65 m   39 m

## PAGES 18–19

### COASTER WORK

1) Ride A takes 24 people, Ride B takes 30, ride C takes 18 and ride D takes 32. So Ride D carries most people per train.
2) Ride D
3) a) 20   b) 15   c) 30   d) 12

### CHALLENGE QUESTION

Ride A can take 480 people
Ride B can take 450 people
Ride C can take 540 people
Ride D can take 384 people

1) So Ride C can take most people per hour.
2) Ride D takes fewest people per hour

## PAGES 20–21

### COASTER WORK

1) a) forty-three metres
   b) one hundred and seventy wooden coasters
   c) nine hundred legs
   d) one thousand two hundred ribbons
   e) one thousand four hundred and forty-one metres
   f) One thousand eight hundred and eighty-two roller coasters
   g) One thousand seven hundred and twelve steel coasters
   h) Three thousand nine hundred items
2) a) 93   b) 308   c) 764   d) 1407 e) 2020
3) 42, 169, 899, 1199, 1440, 1881, 1711, 3899

### CHALLENGE QUESTION

1) a) forty
   b) eight hundred
   c) two
   d) three thousand
   e) seven thousand
   f) fifty thousand
   g) four hundred thousand

2) 144.1, 188.2, 171.2, 390, 2700, 5700, 44 000.

## PAGES 22–23

### COASTER WORK

An estimate between 49 and 54 weeks.

### CHALLENGE QUESTION

1) Depending on your answer for the coaster work you should have an answer between 343 and 407 days.
2) Closest to 1 year.

## PAGES 24–25

### COASTER WORK

1) isosceles triangle    hexagon

   square    pentagon

   hexagon    rectangle

   scalene triangle

2) The scalene triangle, square and rectangle have at least one right angle.
3) The isosceles triangle, the square and the rectangle have at least one line of symmetry.

### CHALLENGE QUESTION

16 small triangles

7 medium sized triangles

3 larger triangles

1 large triangle
Making a total of 27 triangles

## PAGES 26–27

### COASTER WORK

1) a) about 34 m  b) about 29 m   c) 35 m   d) 42 m
2) a) ½ second     b) 12½ seconds
3) a) once         b) 4 times      c) 5 times
   d) 3 times      e) twice

### CHALLENGE QUESTION

1) 58 m, 42 m, 35 m    2) 16 m     3) 7 m
4) a) 25m   b) 15m   c) 35m   d) 25m

# GLOSSARY

**AIRTIME** the word for the "butterflies in your stomach" weightless feeling that you have as you go over a hill.

**BANKING** the tilting on a ride as it goes around a bend.

**BENT** a cross-section of the structure that supports the roller coaster tracks. The metal bars used to make up the bents are called chords diagonals and legs.

**BUNNY HOPS** short fun hills.

**CAMELBACK** a hill that looks like the hump on a camel.

**CAR** a part of the train holding several passsengers.

**CENTRIFUGAL FORCE** the force that pushes something moving in a circle towards the outside edge.

**CROSS-OVER** where one section of the roller coaster crosses over or under another. Often the ride will take you hurtling towards the cross-over, making you think you are going to hit the coaster.

**DOG-LEG RIDE** a straight ride with a turn part way along.

**FRICTION** the way a moving object slows down if it rubs against something else.

**GRAVITY** the force that tends to draw things towards the centre of the earth.

**HYDRAULIC** a mechanism which works by moving liquid.

**LIFT HILL** the first and highest hill of a ride.

**LOOP** a part of the ride that takes passengers completely upside down.

**OUT-AND-BACK RIDE** a ride where you travel along, turn around and then go back.

**RESTRAINT** the harness that secures passengers inside the cars during the ride.

**RIBBONS** thin metal bars connecting bents.

**STEEL ROLLER COASTER** a coaster where the tracks are made out of steel.

**STRUCTURE** the scaffolding that holds the roller coaster up. Both wooden and steel roller coasters can have a metal structure.

**TRAIN** several cars joined together that ride along the path of a roller coaster.

**WOODEN ROLLER COASTER** a coaster where the tracks are made out of wood.

## MATHS GLOSSARY

**ANGLE** – a measure of turn.

**AREA** – the amount of space inside a flat shape. It is measured in squares.

**COORDINATES** – two numbers in brackets used to show position on a grid, such as (3, 2) which means 3 steps to the right and 2 up starting from (0, 0).

**DEGREES** – The units used for measuring angle (written °), or temperature (written °C or °F).

**EQUIVALENT** – having the same value as, for example ½ is equivalent to ¾.

**ESTIMATE** – to find a number or amount that is close to an exact number.

**FIGURES** – digits.

**FRACTIONS** – made when shapes or numbers are split into equal parts. For example, if a shape is cut into 6 equals parts each part is ⅙.

**POLYGON** – a shape with straight sides.

**REVOLUTION** – a complete revolution is one full turn.

**RIGHT ANGLE** – a quarter turn, a turn of 90°.

**SPEED** – a measure of how fast something is moving.

**SUBTRACTION** – taking away one number from another.

### PICTURE CREDITS
Gravity Group: 6-7, 8-9, 10-11, 12-13, 16-17, 20-21, 22-23, 24-25, 26-27
Cedar Point: 1, 14-15, 18-19
Front cover: Getty Images

Every effort has been made to trace the copyright holders, and we apologize in advance for any unintentional omissions.
We would be pleased to insert the appropriate acknowledgements in any subsequent edition of this publication.